The end papers of this year's book show a selection of D.C. Thomson publications that may well have graced the Broons' bookshelves during the 1960s. This was a decade that saw a massive proliferation in published titles, as many popular television shows spawned offshoot books. Thunderbirds, Joe 90, Blue Peter and The Man from U.N.C.L.E., to name but a few, all had their own annuals and sales of such publications reached record levels.

This was reflected in D.C. Thomson's output and the following well-known titles were all launched in the 60s. Bimbo, Diana, Hornet, Judy, Mandy, Adventure, Sparky, Twinkle and Victor will jog the memories of those who lived through this period and spark a frantic search on the internet for those who didn't! The illustration below, taken from the Broons strip in the Sunday Post on October 6th 1963, shows the aftermath of Maw putting the family's reading material down to catch drips from her freshly laundered sheets!

Printed and published in Great Britain by D.C. Thomson & Co., Ltd.,
185 Fleet Street, London EC4A 2HS.
© D.C. Thomson & Co., Ltd., 2004.
ISBN 0851168582

1960-1969

OOR WULLIE 1960-1969

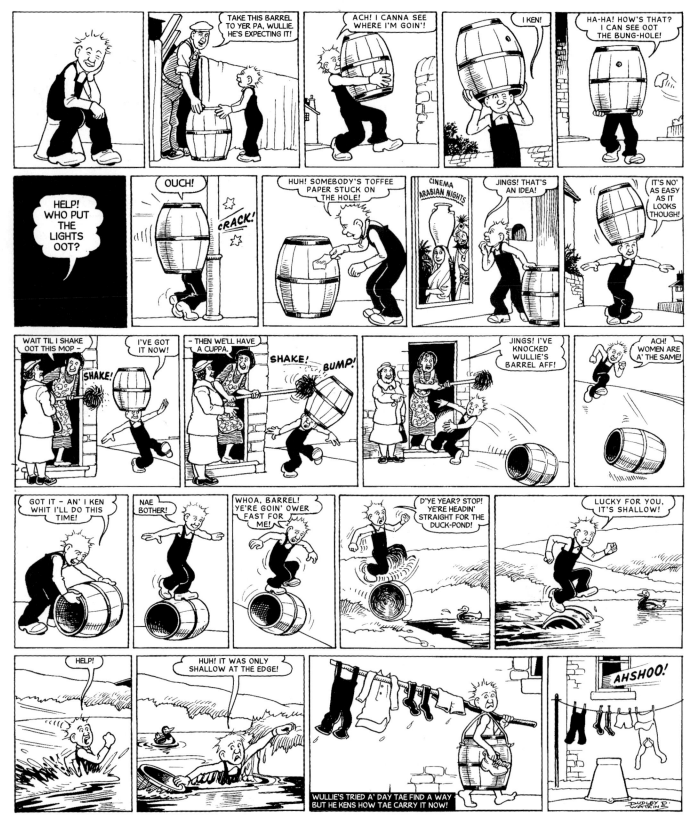

The Sunday Post 10th January 1960

The Sunday Post 10th January 1960

The Sunday Post 17th January 1960

The Sunday Post 17th January 1960

OOR WULLIE 1960-1969

The Sunday Post 7th February 1960

The Sunday Post 20th March 1960

OOR WULLIE 1960-1969

The Sunday Post 3rd April 1960

The Sunday Post 10th April 1960

OOR WULLIE 1960-1969

The Sunday Post 4th September 1960

The Sunday Post 11th September 1960

The Sunday Post 25th December 1960

THE KING OF ROCK ROLLS INTO SCOTLAND!

On the third of March 1960, the King of Rock and Roll, Elvis Presley, set foot on British soil — the first and only occasion he would do so. Returning to America from Germany, where he had spent his two years of national service, Presley stopped off at Prestwick Airport, which at the time was a United States Air Force base. He stayed for a mere two hours but, despite a security clampdown, many of his fans found out he was there and were lucky enough to spend some time in their hero's company. He chatted amiably and signed autographs for those in the crowd — although he must have been bemused at one fan allegedly presenting him with the wrappings of a fish supper to sign!

Later that same year, in December, Andy Stewart, that famed stalwart of the White Heather Club, released the single "Donald Where's yer Troosers?" which reached No. 39 in the charts. In one of the verses the bold Andy sang in the style of Elvis Presley. This reached the ears of the legendary rock 'n' roller who described it as the best impersonation of his voice and singing style he had ever heard!

Sadly, or perhaps thankfully, Elvis never sang any of his many hits in the style of Andy Stewart!

1960-1969

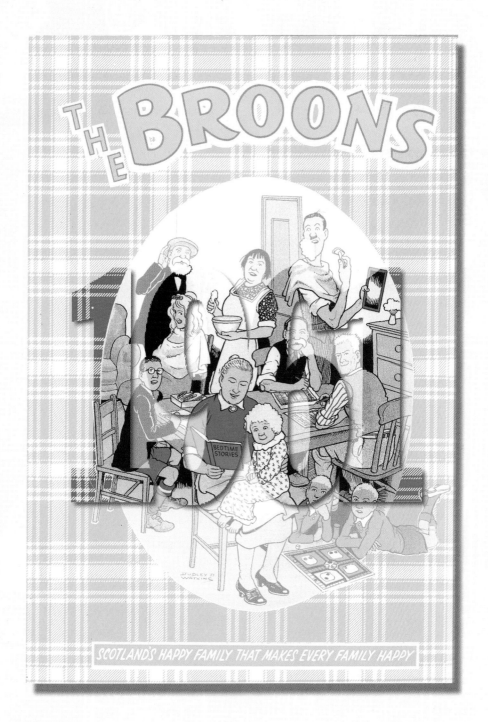

SCOTLAND'S HAPPY FAMILY THAT MAKES EVERY FAMILY HAPPY

OOR WULLIE 1960-1969

The Sunday Post 15th January 1961

The Sunday Post 5th February 1961

The Sunday Post 12th February 1961

OOR WULLIE 1960-1969

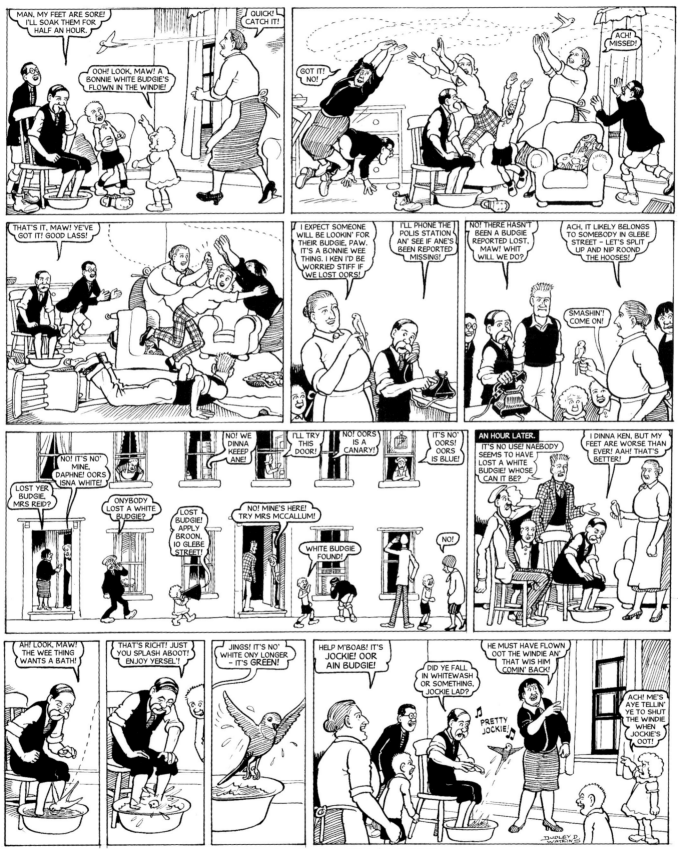

The Sunday Post 23th April 1961

OOR WULLIE 1960-1969

The Sunday Post 18th June 1961

The Sunday Post 21st May 1961

OOR WULLIE 1960-1969

The Sunday Post 9th July 1961

The Sunday Post 18th June 1961

The Sunday Post 31st December 1961

The Sunday Post 17th December 1961

A BOND WITH SCOTLAND!

IN 1962 the first James Bond film, Dr. No, appeared on cinema screens throughout the world. This was the beginning of the most successful movie franchise of all time, with creator Ian Fleming's super spy remaining hugely popular today.

The first actor to play Bond was Thomas Connery, a former milkman and coffin polisher from the Fountainbridge district of Edinburgh.

Big Tam, or Sir Sean Connery as he is now known, was not Ian Fleming's first choice to play his character — he went on record as stating that another Scot, David Niven, would be his preferred actor. However, once the film hit the screens, the actor with the "Scotland Forever" tattoo was immediately embraced by filmgoers as the definitive Bond.

Sean Connery went on to reprise his role as MI5's finest a further five times through to 1971 in From Russia, with Love, Thunderball, You Only Live Twice and Diamonds are Forever. His final outing as 007 came in 1983 with the film Never Say Never Again.

Now a recognised worldwide acting superstar, Connery has left the role that made him famous behind and has a long list of Hollywood hits to his credit. He has never lost his love of his native land and remains both a frequent visitor to, and passionate supporter of Scotland.

1960-1969

OOR WULLIE 1960-1969

The Sunday Post 1st July 1962

OOR WULLIE 1960-1969

The Sunday Post 28th January 1962

The Sunday Post 8th July 1962

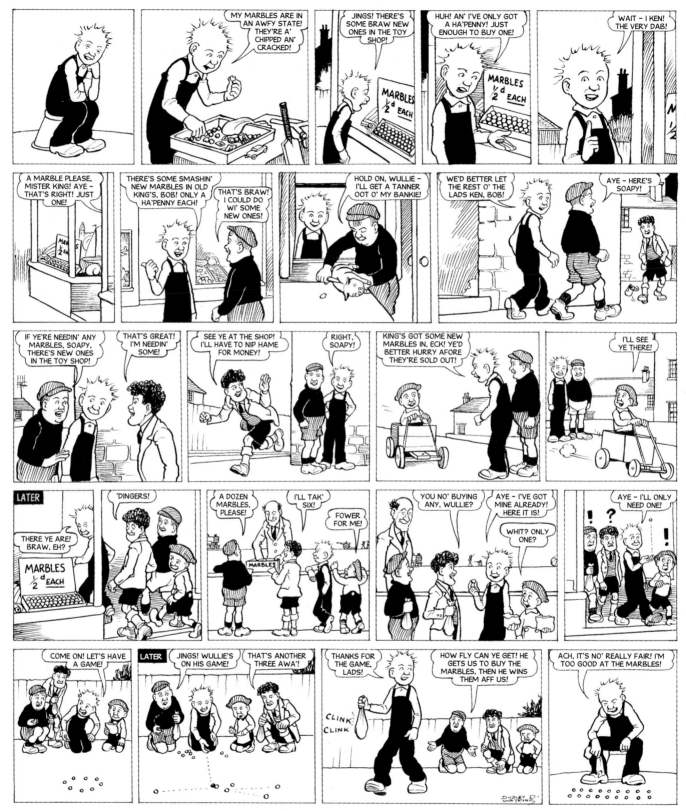

The Sunday Post 5th August 1962

OOR WULLIE 1960-1969

The Sunday Post 8th April 1962

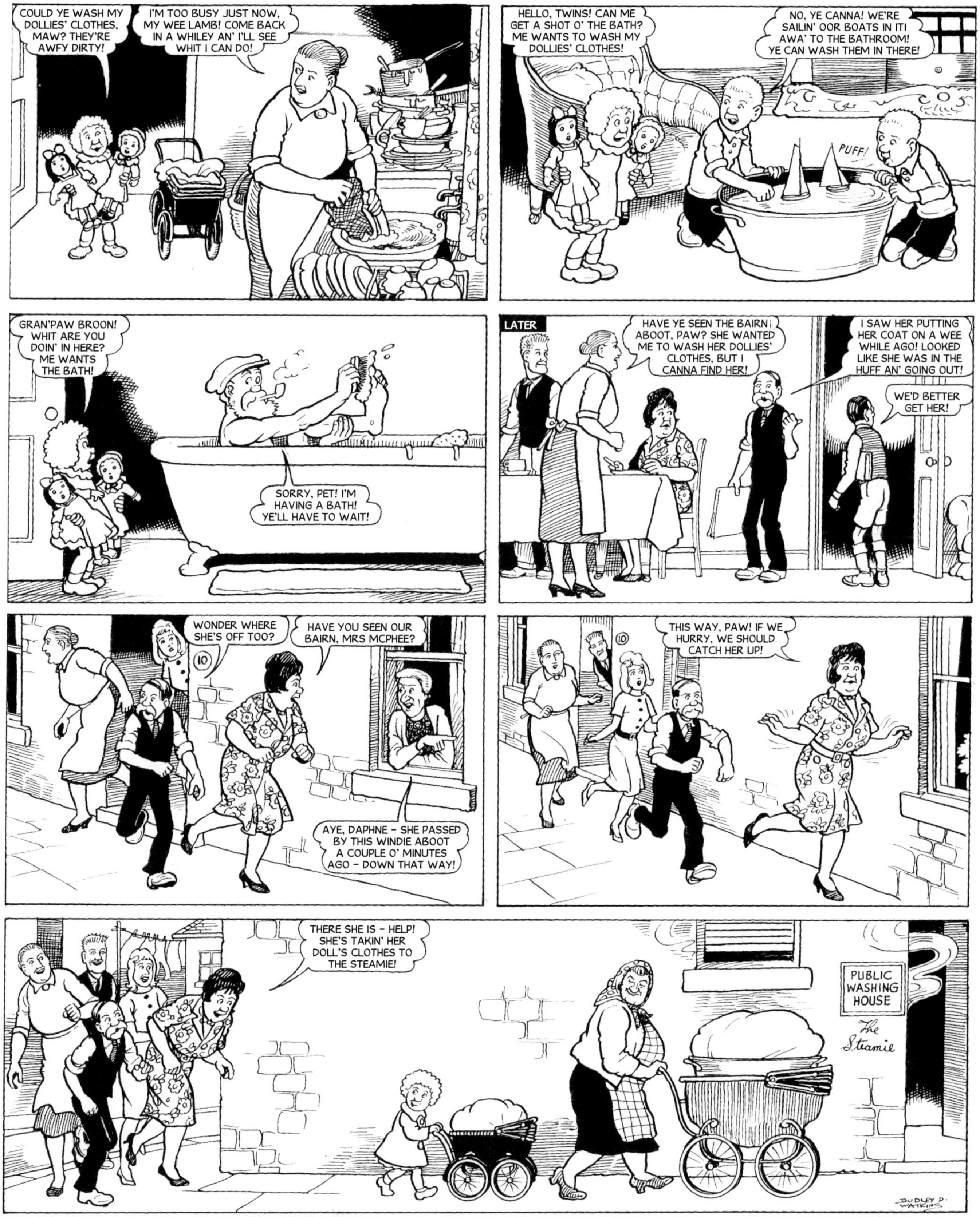

The Sunday Post 16th September 1962

OOR WULLIE 1960-1969

The Sunday Post 10th June 1962

The Sunday Post 14th October 1962

OOR WULLIE 1960-1969

The Sunday Post 12th August 1962

The Sunday Post 18th November 1962

FIFER IN THE FAST LANE

The only son in a family of four daughters, Jim Clark was born in Kilmany, North East Fife, on the fourth of March 1936. Educated in Musselburgh, he later joined the Border Reivers racing team run by Jock McBain.

Jim drove a Lotus Elite in one of his races and made a lasting impression on one Colin Chapman who would one day become his team manager.

After a stint with the Aston Martin team, Jim graduated to the Lotus Formula 1 team. Jim showed potential in his first two seasons before winning his first Grand Prix at Spa, in Belgium, generally regarded as the season's most unforgiving track.

In 1963, Clark won seven of the ten championship races to become World Champion for the first time.

1965 saw him repeat the feat, while also winning at Indianapolis. A fellow Scot, Jackie Stewart, began to emerge as a challenger. Jim's car was plagued by engine problems in 1966, but the next year saw him back in contention, coming third in the rankings.

In 1968 he won in South Africa, over-hauling Juan Manuel Fangio's record of Grand Prix victories. Later that year, in a relatively insignificant Formula 2 race in Hockenheim, the man who declared he would never marry while he continued racing, was killed when his car left the road in the forest circuit. He is still regarded as one of the finest racing drivers of all time.

1960-1969

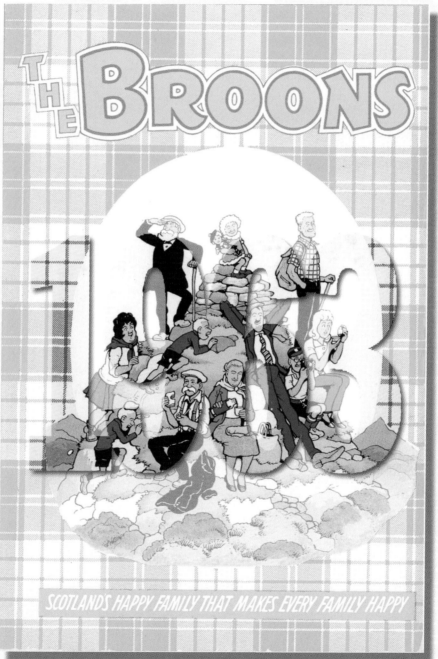

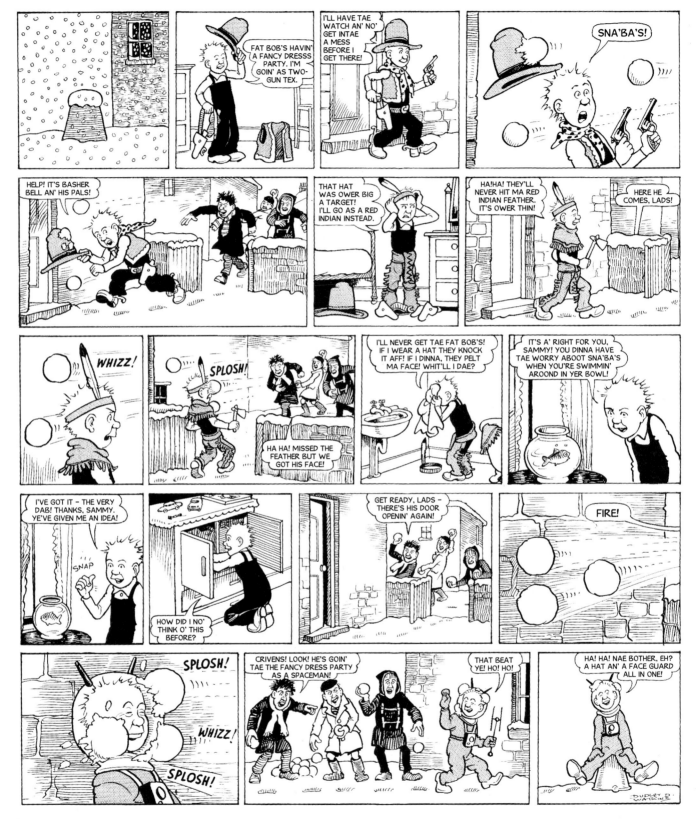

The Sunday Post 6th January 1963

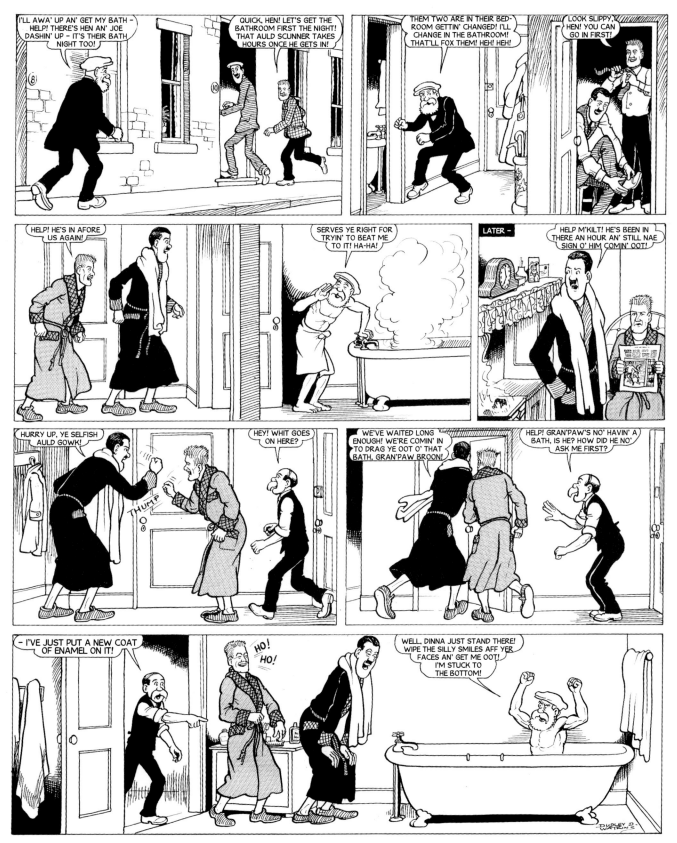

The Sunday Post 3rd March 1963

The Sunday Post 5th May 1963

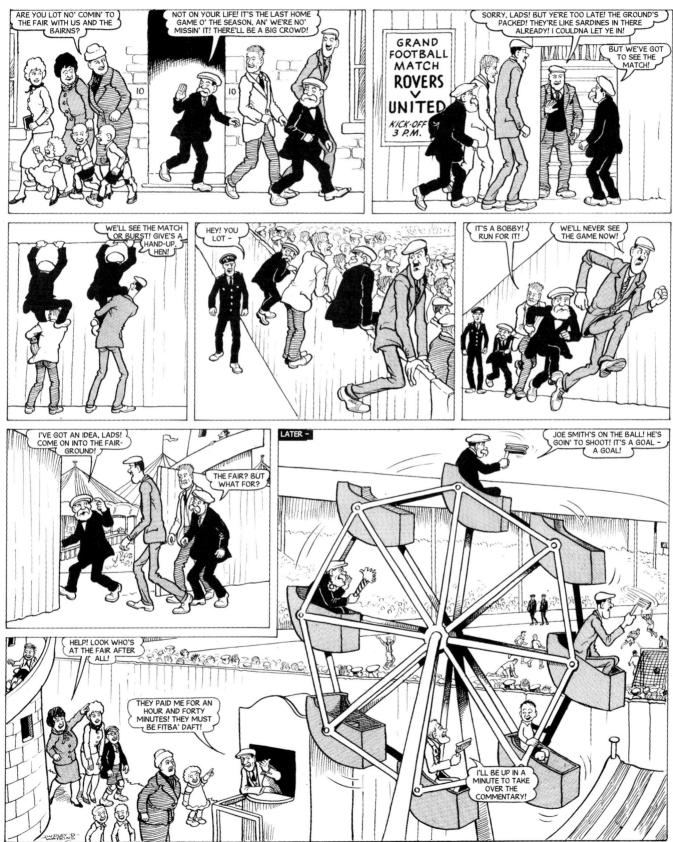

The Sunday Post 12th May 1963

OOR WULLIE 1960-1969

The Sunday Post 9th June 1963

The Sunday Post 19th May 1963

OOR WULLIE 1960-1969

The Sunday Post 18th August 1963

The Sunday Post 26th May 1963

OOR WULLIE 1960-1969

The Sunday Post 22nd September 1963

The Sunday Post 30th June 1963

OOR WULLIE 1960-1969

The Sunday Post 22nd December 1963

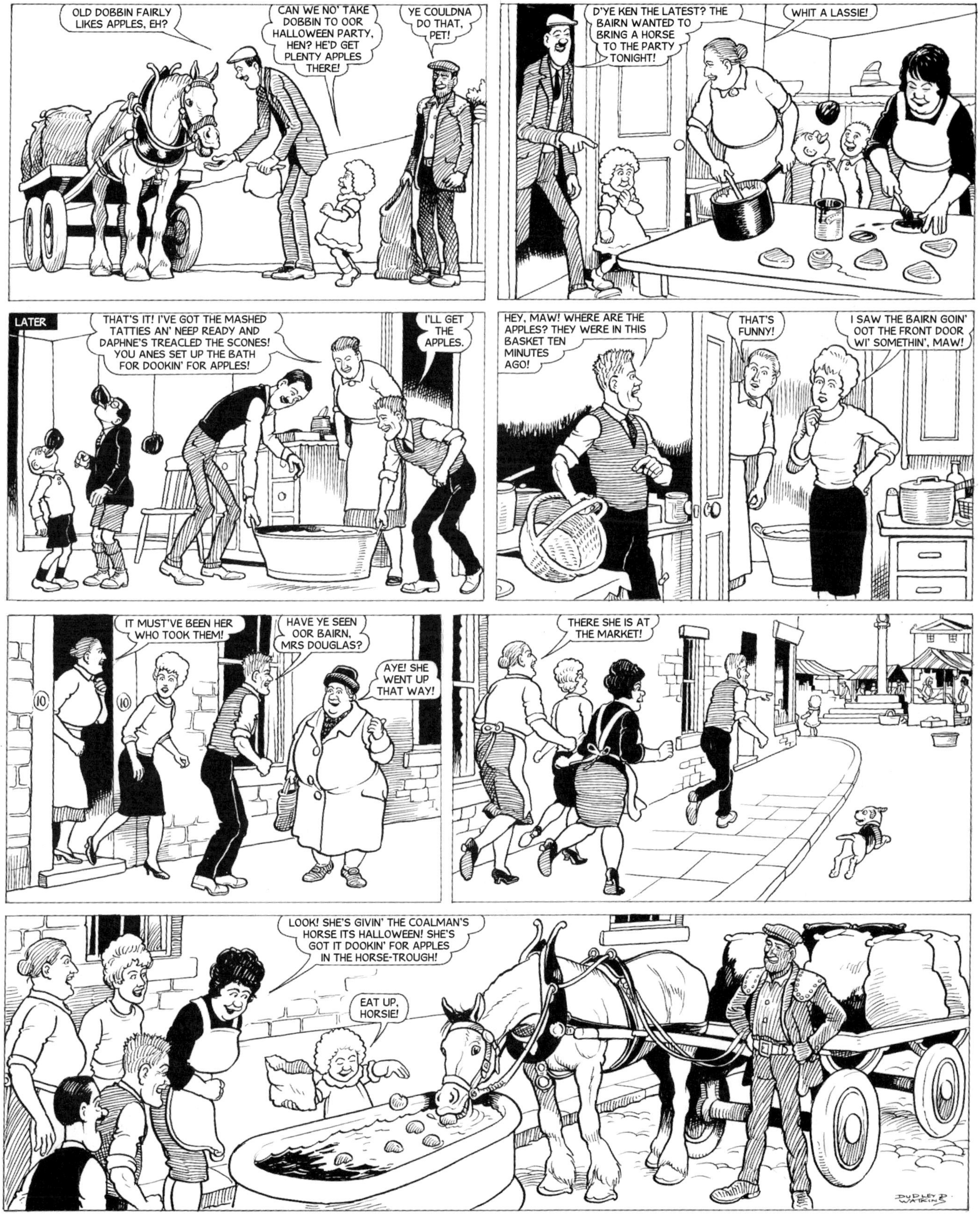

The Sunday Post 27th October 1963

FAREWELL TO THE FERRIES

On the 4th of September 1964, the regular ferry service between North and South Queensferry, which had been in place for 800 years, ceased. In its place was the longest suspension bridge in Europe, the Forth Road Bridge.

The pressure on the ferries was great. One and a half million people used the service every year, and at night or in severe weather the lengthy detour to the Kincardine Bridge was the alternative.

HER MAJESTY THE QUEEN
ACCOMPANIED BY
HIS ROYAL HIGHNESS
THE DUKE OF EDINBURGH
FIRST CROSSED THIS BRIDGE
4TH SEPTEMBER 1964

THE QUEENSFERRY PASSAGE
NAMED AFTER QUEEN MARGARET
WAS THUS SUPERSEDED AFTER
EIGHT HUNDRED YEARS
OF CONTINUAL USE

Established in 1947, the Forth Road Bridge Joint Board was given responsibility for the construction of the bridge. The Edinburgh Corporation, the County Councils of Fife and West Lothian, and the Town Councils of Kirkcaldy and Dunfermline comprised the original members of the board.

Construction work began on the bridge and its approaches in 1958. The one and a half miles long bridge, cost just under twenty million pounds to build. Fourteen million of this figure has been repaid.

When Queen Elizabeth opened the bridge in 1964, four million vehicles crossed the bridge annually. That traffic flow has now increased to a yearly figure of twenty three million.

It would be interesting to know if anyone recognises any of the vehicle registration plates in the photograph taken at the bridge tolls in 1964.

1960-1969

OOR WULLIE 1960-1969

The Sunday Post 12th January 1964

THE BROONS 1960-1969

The Sunday Post 26th January 1964

OOR WULLIE 1960-1969

The Sunday Post 9th February 1964

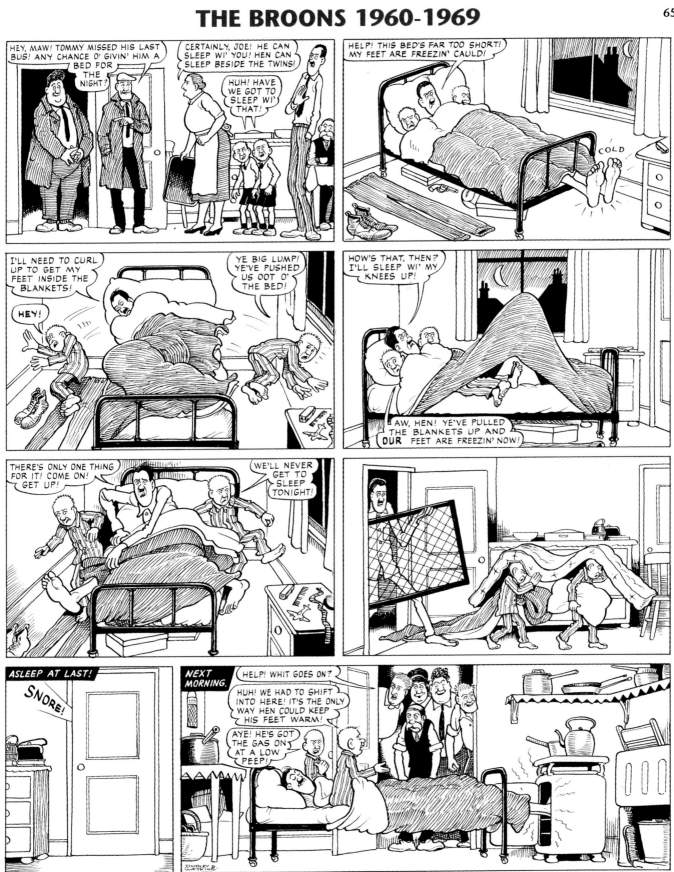

The Sunday Post 8th March 1964

OOR WULLIE 1960-1969

The Sunday Post 5th April 1964

OOR WULLIE 1960-1969

The Sunday Post 23rd August 1964

The Sunday Post 18th October 1964

OOR WULLIE 1960-1969

The Sunday Post 6th September 1964

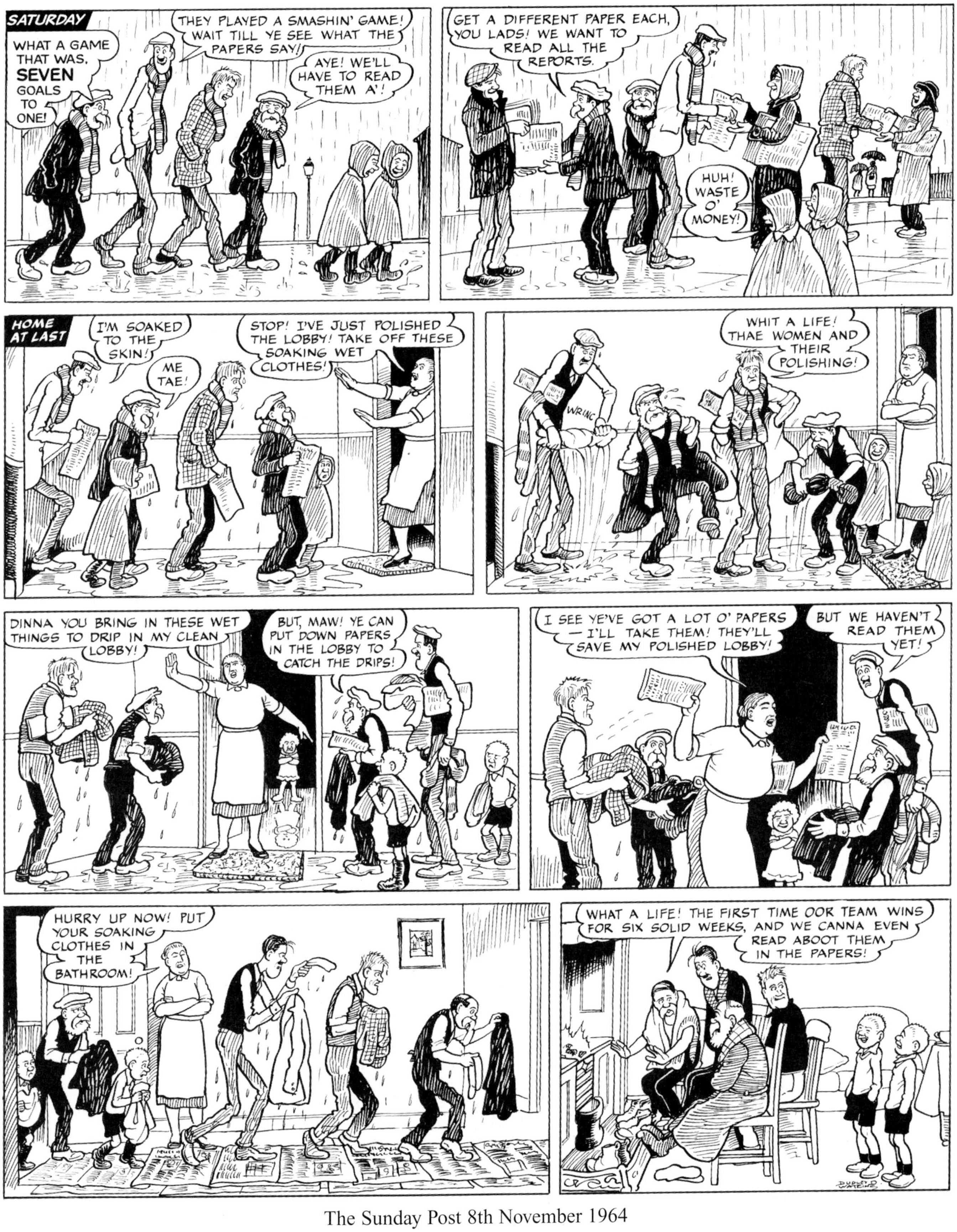

The Sunday Post 8th November 1964

OOR WULLIE 1960-1969

The Sunday Post 13th December 1964

FLOWER POWER! (OF SCOTLAND)

If there is one thing that defines the 1960s as a decade it is the music. Flower power, psychedelia and the hippy movement are all synonymous with the time. At the forefront of this musical revolution was Scotland's own Donovan. Born Donovan Leitch in a Maryhill tenement in Glasgow, the talented teenage musician sprang to prominence with his 1965 release "Catch the Wind". Marketed as Britain's answer to the legendary Bob Dylan, Donovan enjoyed huge popularity with hits such as Jenifer Juniper, Mellow Yellow and Sunshine Superman. Donovan later toured with the aforementioned Bob Dylan as well as Joan Baez and received both critical and audience acclaim at the 1965 Newport Folk Festival in Rhode Island.

Donovan certainly embodied the spirit of the times embracing as he did vegetarianism and Buddhist and Hindu philosophies as well as becoming a student of the Maharishi Mahesh Yogi. In 1969 he married Linda Lawrence, the widow of former Rolling Stones member Brian Jones. The couple have two children, Donovan Leitch Jnr., a successful model and musician who married Scots model Kirsty Hume in 1997, and Ione Skye the actress.

1960-1969

OOR WULLIE 1960-1969

The Sunday Post 10th January 1965

The Sunday Post 21st March 1965

OOR WULLIE 1960-1969

The Sunday Post 14th February 1965

The Sunday Post 4th April 1965

OOR WULLIE 1960-1969

The Sunday Post 4th April 1965

The Sunday Post 2nd May 1965

OOR WULLIE 1960-1969

The Sunday Post 20th June 1965

The Sunday Post 6th June 1965

OOR WULLIE 1960-1969

The Sunday Post 24th October 1965

The Sunday Post 4th July 1965

OOR WULLIE 1960-1969

The Sunday Post 7th November 1965

The Sunday Post 14th November 1965

VITAL VIEWING

IN 1905, Neil Munro, Editor-in-Chief of the Glasgow Evening News, began penning stories of Para Handy, the canny skipper of the Clyde puffer, The Vital Spark.

Para Handy first reached the screens in 1959, but in 1965, The Vital Spark made a successful appearance in the Comedy Playhouse programmes.

On the 28th of January, 1966, Series One began, featuring Roddy McMillan as Para Handy, Walter Carr as Dougie, John Grieve as the never-cheerful Dan McPhail, and Alex McAvoy as Sunny Jim. Co-incidentally, the adventures of the puffer, fast becoming an anachronism, manned by its crew who came into frequent conflict with authority, dovetailed nicely into the anti-establishment mood of the times, and the series was a great success.

The puffer itself, in reality called The Saxon, was built in 1903.

Neil Munro, from Inverary, wished to be known as a serious author, and published a number of novels and poetry, but will be best remembered for the unforgettable characters he created, aboard the good ship, The Vital Spark.

OOR WULLIE 1960-1969

The Sunday Post 2nd January 1966

The Sunday Post 19th June 1966

OOR WULLIE 1960-1969

The Sunday Post 13th February 1966

The Sunday Post 28th August 1966

OOR WULLIE 1960-1969

The Sunday Post 20th March 1966

The Sunday Post 9th October 1966

OOR WULLIE 1960-1969

The Sunday Post 5th June 1966

The Sunday Post 6th November 1966

OOR WULLIE 1960-1969

The Sunday Post 7th August 1966

The Sunday Post 4th December 1966

OOR WULLIE 1960-1969

The Sunday Post 20th November 1966

The Sunday Post 25th December 1966

PIRATES IN THE FORTH

AT one minute past midnight, on the first day of 1966, a pirate radio ship based in the Firth of Forth, began to broadcast.

Paul Young was the first voice on Radio

Scotland, launching what was to become the Central Belt's most listened to radio station.

The station specialised in playing the music of the sixties generation, music that the land based stations had failed to provide.

Due to an initial lack of funds the programmes were anarchic, yet it was this very approach that struck a chord in their young audience.

The station even spawned its own magazine, entitled "242".

Time was running out for the pirate stations, and in March 1967 the station was fined for broadcasting illegally.

The converted lighthouse ship, The Comet, continued broadcasting from Fife Ness then Belfast, but when the Marine Offences Bill was approved in August the broadcasting ceased.

The pirates left a lasting legacy, however, with Radio One being dedicated to playing the popular songs of the day.

1960-1969

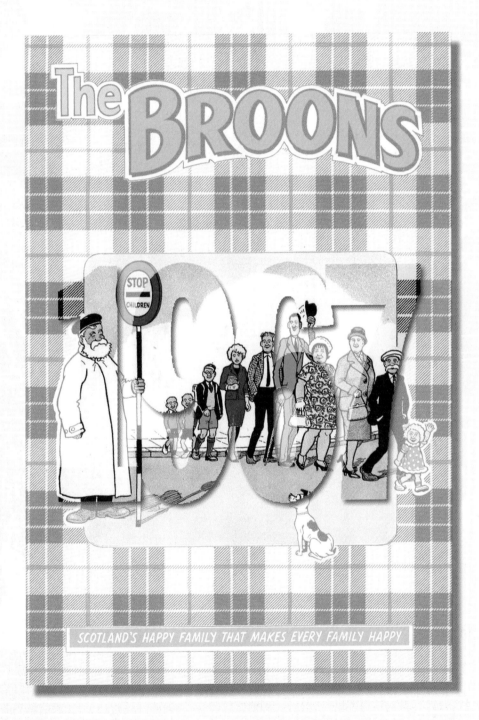

OOR WULLIE 1960-1969

The Sunday Post 15th January 1967

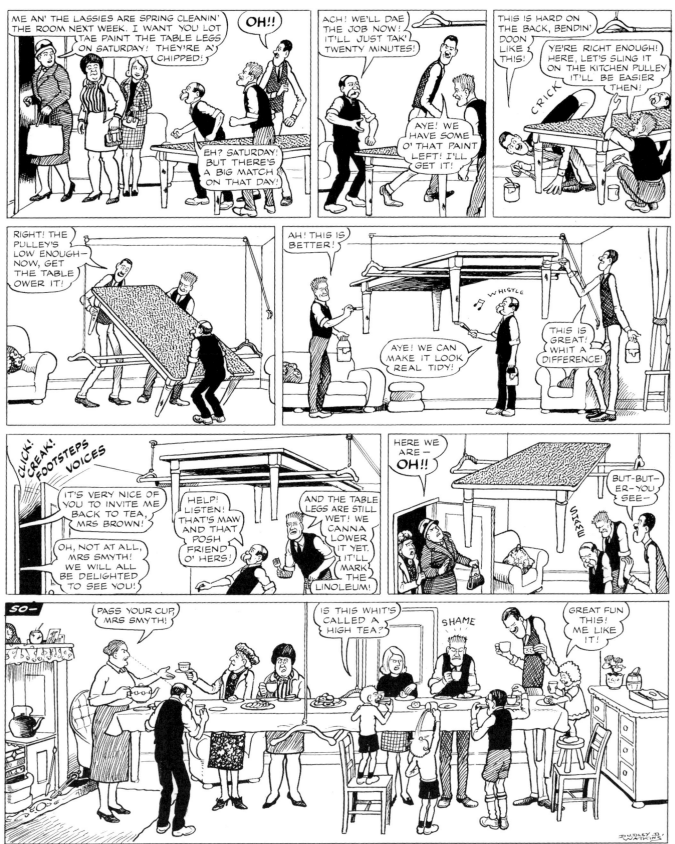

The Sunday Post 23rd April 1967

OOR WULLIE 1960-1969

The Sunday Post 5th February 1967

The Sunday Post 28th May 1967

OOR WULLIE 1960-1969

The Sunday Post 16th July 1967

The Sunday Post 2nd July 1967

OOR WULLIE 1960-1969

The Sunday Post 23rd July 1967

The Sunday Post 23rd July 1967

OOR WULLIE 1960-1969

The Sunday Post 13th August 1967

The Sunday Post 3rd September 1967

OOR WULLIE 1960-1969

The Sunday Post 5th November 1967

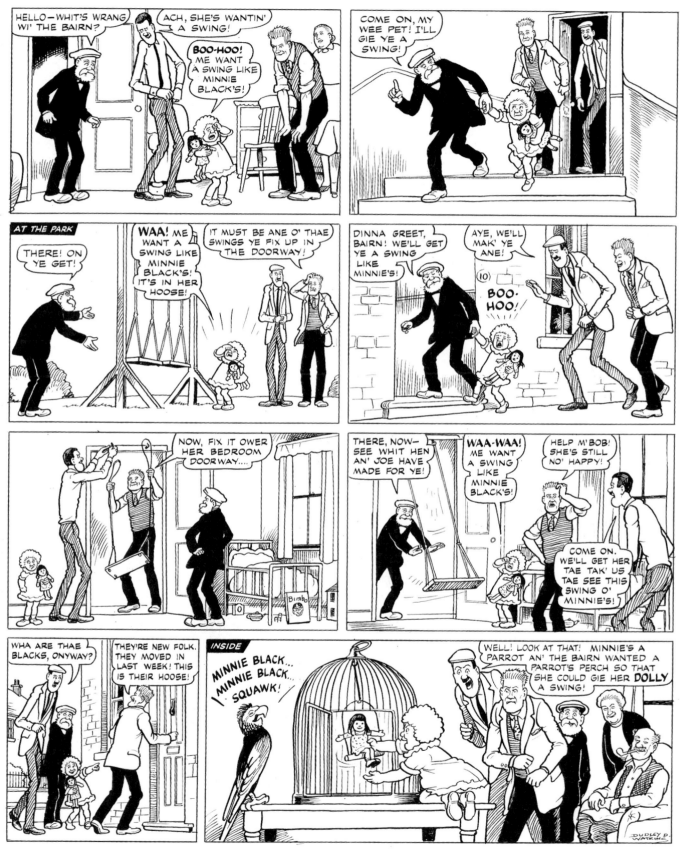

The Sunday Post 1st October 1967

BUSBY'S BRILLIANCE

IN May 1968, at Wembley, Manchester United became the first English side to win the European Champions' Trophy. This success followed on from Scottish champions Celtic becoming the first British winners the previous year. In common with Celtic's Jock Stein, Manchester United had a Scottish manager in Bellshill-born Matt Busby. An international wing-half, Busby had played at both Manchester City and Liverpool before being offered the manager's job at Old Trafford in 1945, at the age of 36.

Busby was a real tracksuit manager, spending a lot of time on the training ground rearing young, homegrown players. He peppered his teams with only a handful of players bought from other clubs. His young team were christened the 'Busby Babes' and enjoyed tremendous domestic success before becoming the first English side to enter the European Cup in 1958. Tragically, after the Munich Air Disaster, many supremely talented young players were lost.

Busby, who himself only just survived, began the long process of rebuilding his team. Fellow Munich survivor Bobby Charlton, along with George Best and Denis Law became the most-feared attacking trio of their era. Although by 1968 this team was ageing, and Denis Law was missing from the final through injury, hopes were high that Manchester United could defeat the mighty Benfica side, which included the legendary Eusebio.

With the score at 1-1 after ninety minutes, Graca having equalised Charlton's opener, extra-time loomed. United took command, however, and with goals from Best, Kidd and Charlton again, they ran out 4-1 victors to fulfil Busby's dream.

In recognition of his achievements, Matt Busby was knighted that same year.

1960-1969

OOR WULLIE 1960-1969

The Sunday Post 14th January 1968

The Sunday Post 24th March 1968

OOR WULLIE 1960-1969

The Sunday Post 28th January 1968

The Sunday Post 21st July 1968

OOR WULLIE 1960-1969

Clearly Ravioli was regarded as the height of culinary adventurousness in 1968.

The Sunday Post 30th June 1968

The Sunday Post 11th August 1968

The Sunday Post 15th September 1968

The Sunday Post 27th October 1968

OOR WULLIE 1960-1969

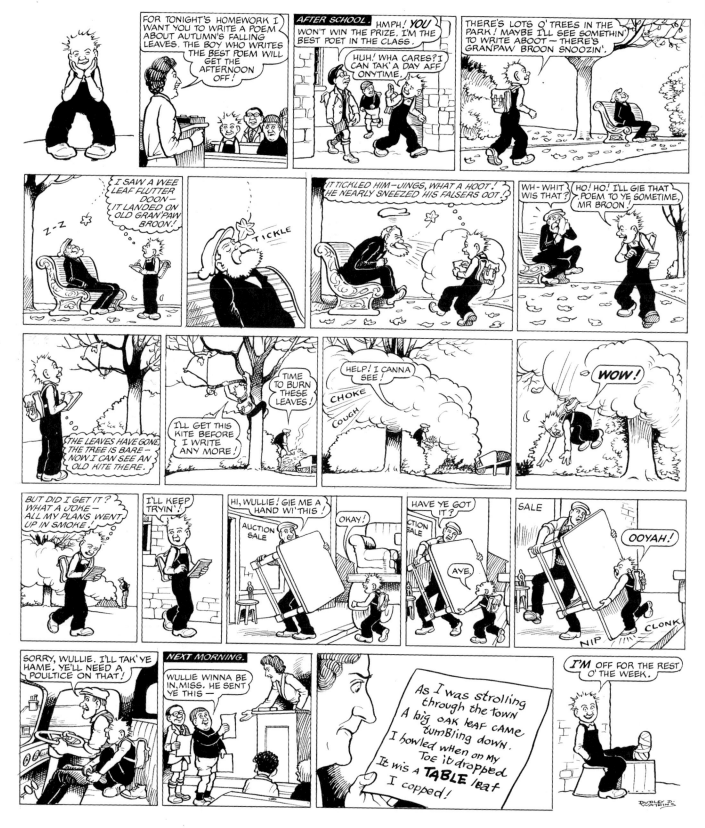

The Sunday Post 29th September 1968

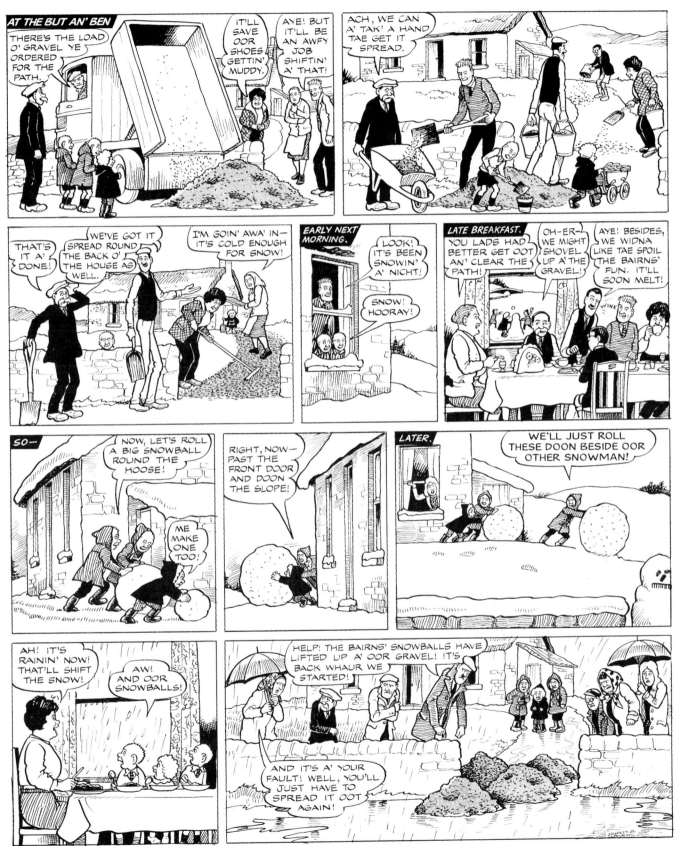

The Sunday Post 17th November 1968

OOR WULLIE 1960-1969

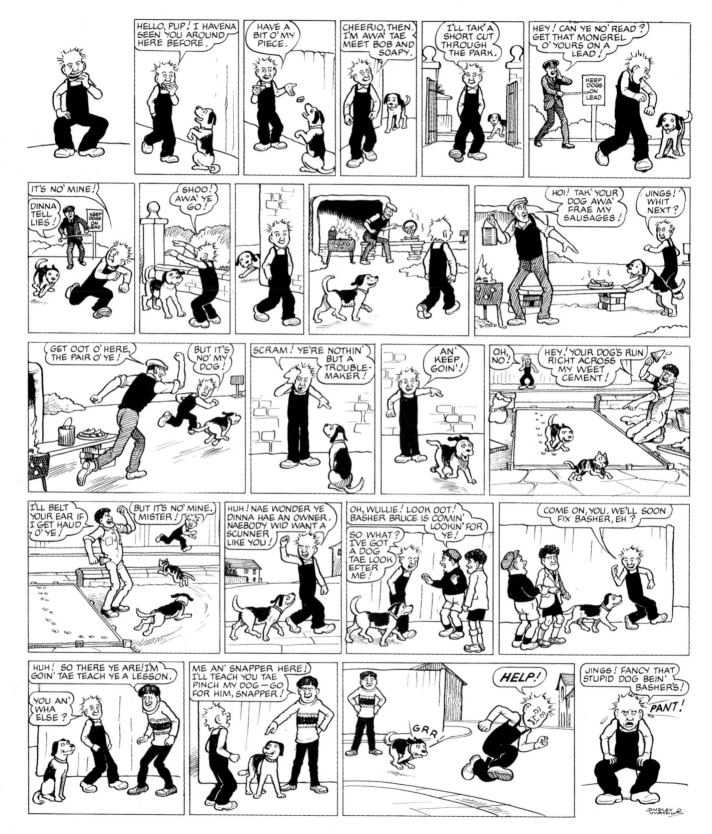

The Sunday Post 24th November 1968

The Sunday Post 8th December 1968

BROWN'S BATTLERS

Born in Edinburgh on February 15th, 1925, Eric Brown found himself as Captain of Great Britain and Ireland's Ryder Cup team, facing the awesome challenge of taking on the cream of the United States' golfers over the Royal Birkdale course.

Six of the British team were chosen purely on tournament results but the team captain was allowed to select a further six at his own discretion. He chose up and coming players, including two Scots, Brian Barnes and Bernard Gallacher.

Brown immediately raised the stakes by instructing his team not to look for any American balls that were lost in the rough.

In the morning of the first day, Brown began and ended his selection with experienced players, trusting to youth in the middle order.

Britain went in leading four and a half to three and a half.

The match continued to be fiercely fought and surrounded in controversy.

On the fourth day, the final match would decide the Ryder Cup. Jack Nicklaus famously conceded Tony Jacklin's tricky putt and the match was tied.

Although the United States had retained the trophy, Sam Snead allowed it to remain in Britain for a year.

Eric Brown hoped that future Ryder Cup teams would incorporate overseas players to keep the matches competitive. never have to

1960-1969

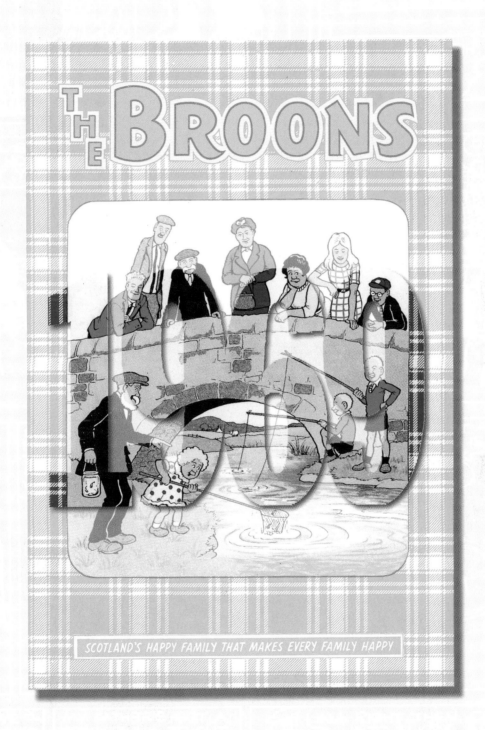

OOR WULLIE 1960-1969

The Sunday Post 26th January 1969

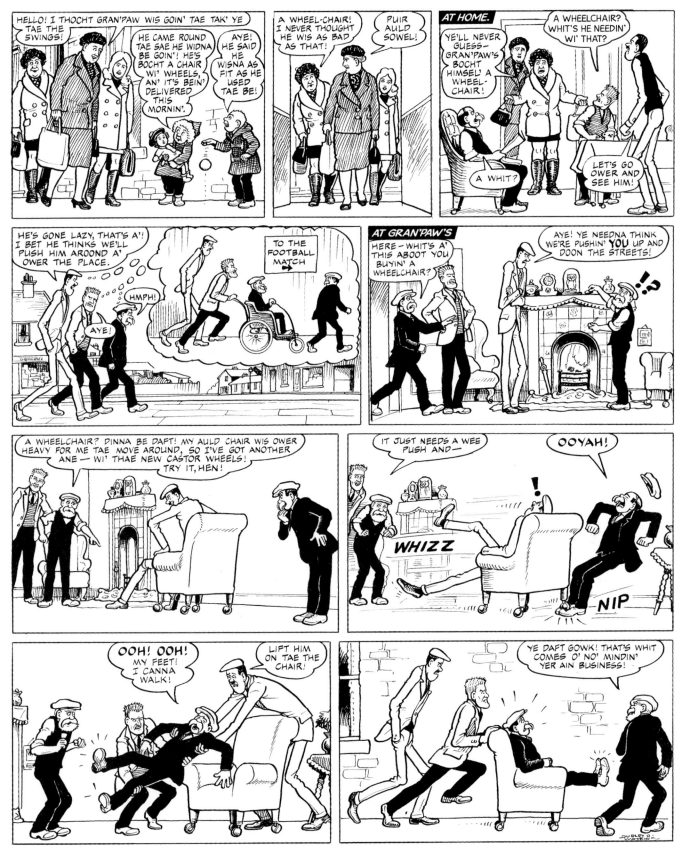

The Sunday Post 5th January 1969

OOR WULLIE 1960-1969

The Sunday Post 11th May 1969

The Sunday Post 2nd February 1969

OOR WULLIE 1960-1969

The Sunday Post 1st June 1969

The Sunday Post 23rd February 1969

OOR WULLIE 1960-1969

The Sunday Post 15th June 1969

The Sunday Post 6th July 1969

OOR WULLIE 1960-1969

The Sunday Post 13th July 1969

The Sunday Post 27th July 1969